COLLECT, CREATE, AND CELEBRATE

Pin Game Strong

YOUR ULTIMATE ENAMEL PIN COLLECTION

COLLECT, CREATE, AND CELEBRATE

Pin Game Strong

YOUR ULTIMATE ENAMEL PIN COLLECTION

EDUARDO MORALES

INSIGHT EDITIONS

San Rafael, California

Contents

stay woke.

FAKE

TOO PRETTY FOR THIS SHIT

DAMN GOOD JOE

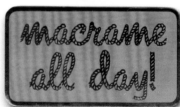

macramé all day!

MY GOD YOU SUCK

The Pin Game
INTRODUCTION

The humble enamel pin is now a cultural phenomenon. New pins of every design and color imaginable have popped up on jackets, backpacks, purses, and lapels all over the world. They have been the subjects of numerous trend pieces and are eagerly sought-after collectibles at tons of conventions and events.

My personal journey into enamel pin obsession began back in spring 2015 when I started an enamel-pin-dedicated Instagram account, @pinlord. I am not a designer, I had no experience producing anything of any kind, and I wasn't particularly entrepreneurial before starting it. A few years later, @pinlord is the largest social media page exclusively focused on promoting enamel pins made by independent sellers from all over the world. It's visited by thousands of people every day, and I feel blessed to be able to make a full-time living from it.

I've been lucky to play a small role in the pin movement, and I'm glad I can share my enthusiasm. The book you're holding is not the definitive chronicle of the enamel pin collection and creation universe, known as the "pin game." It isn't about any particular group of people or any specific set of pin designs. This book is one account of pin obsession, told through my eyes and aimed at documenting a handful of the most inspiring pins, anecdotes, and insights that the movement has to offer. It's meant to celebrate the people who express themselves through the art of pin making and honor those who support it. What makes this community unique is that anyone can be a part of it and that all designs are special in their own ways. I hope the photos and stories here inspire you the same way they've inspired me.

10/10 WOULD NOT RECOMMEND

MEMES

SUPERTRAMP BREAKFAST IN AMERICA IS THE BEST RECORD IN THE HISTORY OF MANKIND.

there are no mistakes only happy accidents

STAY

DEATH BEFORE DECAF

CHILL

PERMANENT RESIDENT SAN JUNIPERO

FAKE NEWS!

stay woke.

A Brief History of
THE PIN CRAZE

Enamel pins have a long history. You may have come across them in your dad's old drawer, at a vintage thrift store, or in a tourist-trap gift shop. Like postage stamps, vintage toys, or trading cards, enamel pins have been a collector favorite for decades given their ease of storage, depth and breadth of designs available, and tendency to increase in value over time. But unlike collecting enamel pins, making them has not always been an easily accessible endeavor.

Traditionally, information on the topic has been scarce, access to factories limited, costs high, and distribution channels mostly unavailable to small, independent makers. Enamel pins have historically been produced and distributed by large, established organizations, brands, and corporations with the intent of selling products or communicating particular messages.

Luckily for us, that all changed when the internet—and more importantly, social media—came along. The internet empowered a new generation of creative types to express themselves and forever changed the way we create and collect enamel pins. For myself and many other early pin enthusiasts, the pin-collection obsession started when we first discovered @patchgame on Instagram. Although the name might appear misleading at first, many credit that page as the main catalyst for the wide popularization of pins on social media, in turn leading to the proliferation of the independent makers who characterize this DIY movement.

In the fall of 2014, New Zealander Padraig Simpson started @patchgame to showcase some of his favorite patch designs and photos from his personal collection to friends, family, and anyone else interested in the topic. As one of the first Instagram accounts solely dedicated to promoting unique merchandise by independent makers, @patchgame quickly became the go-to hub for a small but rapidly growing group of rogue DIY-ers interested in connecting with like-minded people as well as finding other makers' latest designs. To identify themselves and find others, enthusiasts started using the #patchgame hashtag in their posts. The term quickly became the self-identifying name the community rallied around. The hashtag #patchgamestrong developed for those with fierce obsessions with making and collecting patches.

By winter of that year, @patchgame's audience was in the thousands, and a featured post on the account usually led to significant sales for the tagged seller. It was around this time that Simpson recalls a significant wave of new pins entering the Instagram DIY scene:

"Around November 2014, the makers featured on @patchgame were able to sell a few items due to the posts on my page, and as a thank you, they would send a patch as well as some new products they were testing in their shops, like enamel pins and stickers. There were a handful of brands and artists, like Valley Cruise Press, Big Bud Press, Pintrill, Prize NYC, Mean Folk, Explorer's Press, Sara Lyons, Adam J. Kurtz, Tuesday Bassen, and a few others that had been creating unique pins for a while, but it wasn't until the winter of 2014 that I saw a noticeable increase in the number of independent makers creating pins and patches. And by independent makers, I mean people with no specific art or business background, just regular people creating one-off designs out of their homes. In January of 2015, I started testing the first enamel pin posts on @patchgame, using the #pingame hashtag to differentiate them from my regular #patchgame features."

From then on, the enamel-pin-focused segment of the community began using the #pingame hashtag in their photos to show off the latest enamel pin designs, and like the #patchgame hashtag before it, #pingame became the label this new movement of independent enamel pin makers rallied around and made their own. How "pin game strong" you were depended on your level of obsession with making and collecting pins.

FOR MYSELF AND MANY OTHER EARLY PIN ENTHUSIASTS, THE PIN-COLLECTION OBSESSION STARTED WHEN WE FIRST DISCOVERED @PATCHGAME ON INSTAGRAM.

Social media tools like Instagram had made it free, fun, and simple for anyone to reach large audiences that were previously inaccessible to independent makers. In combination with access to quick, reliable, and affordable production from Chinese factories that became open to small orders from US-based clients and available to contact through third-party services like Alibaba or Google, no longer did people need design and production backgrounds or big budgets. For the first time ever, anyone with internet access and a smartphone could design, produce, and sell enamel pins for less than $200. The drastic lowering of the barrier to entry fostered an explosion of growth and renaissance in pin design.

BY SUMMER 2015, PEOPLE FROM ALL WALKS OF LIFE AND ALL OVER THE WORLD WERE DISCOVERING THE PIN GAME, MAKING PINS OF THEIR OWN AND SHARING THEM ON INSTAGRAM.

By summer 2015, people from all walks of life and all over the world were discovering the pin game, making pins of their own and sharing them on Instagram. Simpson recalls:

"I was getting twenty to two hundred messages a day from people requesting a post for their pins. Several of the makers who were just starting back then are now very successful pin sellers. It was amazing to witness so many new designs of all types, shapes, and colors being created every single day by people who were passionate about sharing their ideas with the world. It was also during this time when some of the first independent makers were earning enough to survive from their enamel pin businesses alone. In my case, it was September of 2015 when I started to make a decent income from promoting posts on @patchgame. While at work [at my regular job], my boss kept warning me about using my phone. After a few weeks I told him, 'This phone pays more than you do, see ya later.' It's been a couple of years since then, and I'm still lucky enough to be able to make my living from enamel pins because of the people who love and support the movement."

The rapid pace at which new makers and enthusiasts have discovered enamel pins has only multiplied since then. By the time this book is published, tens of thousands of one-of-a-kind designs will have been created since the early days of the pin game, with hundreds of thousands more to come.

INSPIRATION

The pin game is a badass community of collectors, enthusiasts, and artists who share a passion for enamel pins, especially those created by independent designers. The beauty of this hobby/obsession is you don't need to be a professional to make and share your distinctive creations.

In this book, we document and celebrate the unique designs that characterize the pin game and the stories behind their creators. Every person featured here started with nothing but an idea of an awesome pin and the passion to put it out into the world. Here are a few of their stories.

"WHEN PEOPLE CONNECT WITH MY ART, I FEEL MORE CONNECTED TO THE WORLD AND IT MAKES MY HEART HAPPY."

—Serena Epstein, Oh Plesiosaur

MORGAN WATT

Inner Decay

"It sounds kind of funny to say, but the difference in my life before and after I started designing pins is like night and day. I was living in NYC and had just quit my day job to be a stay-at-home dad when I started Inner Decay. I put $150 into production of my own money, and since then the company has been self-sustaining. Within three months I was grossing more than I had been making at my previous job. Within a year, my wife was able to quit her job and start a company of her own. Within two years we were able to purchase a home, and we both now run our businesses full-time. So pins truly gave us our independence in work and life to make some big decisions. It's scary sometimes and it's definitely not the lifestyle for everyone, but if you're a self-motivating, creative person, then being an entrepreneur definitely has its benefits."

CHIANG PINKNEY

Lady Love Letter

"I started Lady Love Letter as a personal distraction from my struggle with depression and anxiety. The distraction has now become therapy for me. I receive a lot of love and support from the pin community when I'm feeling my lowest. It has been a beacon of unwavering light and a sign of hope for me. Lady Love Letter has also immersed me back into art, my first love. It has helped me find myself again."

YULIYA VELIGURSKAYA

Studiocult.co

"Upon graduating from college with a BS in architecture, I found myself sort of disappointed and creatively restricted by the field. It was about 5 percent design and 95 percent paperwork. Entering the pin game allowed me to start my own design studio, where I plan to design not only pins but also housewares, clothing, merchandise, and furniture. Designing pins has been a sort of lowest-barrier-to-entry way to create a product that is completely custom, affordable to manufacture, and easy to distribute due to its size. This gave me the control that I really wanted over my work."

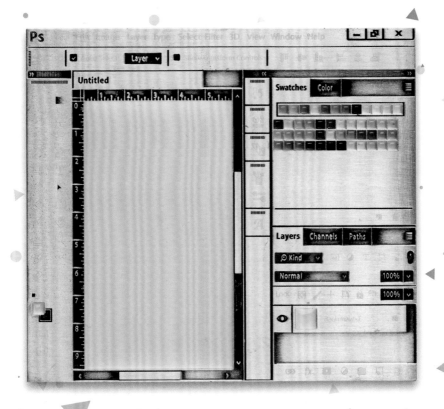

MAX MCKENNA

Roll the Vice

"When I began collecting pins, I realized that it was an affordable way to support artists directly. Art is the force that defines culture and makes humans so profoundly beautiful and different from every other species on this planet. It is an intrinsic part of everything we do, love, and feel. Support pin makers, support artists, support creativity, and therein, support culture."

CHARLIE WAGERS

Lost Lust Supply

"[Here's] one exciting story, and one ridiculous, that happened to us since we've been selling pins. First, within two months of being in business, we were cold-called by a buyer from Urban Outfitters to stock our pins worldwide. And another time we shipped pins to Jimmy Buffett! Hilariously, he got two of our beach-themed pins. Every bit of the journey has been a wild ride."

SERENA EPSTEIN

Oh Plesiosaur

"Pins have provided an accessible, portable form for my art, making it easy for me to reach a wider audience and send so much more of my art out into the world. Scientists who study vampire squid have bought my vampire squid pin, students have surprised their science teachers with my 'Science is Real' pin, and members of the LGBTQ+ community have worn my queer pins to marches and rallies. When people connect with my art, I feel more connected to the world and it makes my heart happy."

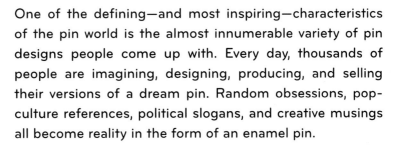

A World of
PINS

One of the defining—and most inspiring—characteristics of the pin world is the almost innumerable variety of pin designs people come up with. Every day, thousands of people are imagining, designing, producing, and selling their versions of a dream pin. Random obsessions, pop-culture references, political slogans, and creative musings all become reality in the form of an enamel pin.

Cat pins, pizza pins, art pins, political pins, pins about your favorite TV show from the '90s, a pin about that one obscure character you're obsessed with from that cult indie movie you've watched a hundred times, pins about where you come from, pins about important cultural movements, pins about being sad, pins about being happy, and even pins about absolutely nothing. They're all unique in their own way, and like the internet itself, half the fun comes from just exploring what's out there.

In this section of the book, we'll explore just a sample of the most popular, obscure, extreme, and random types of pins, told through the people making them.

If you had the opportunity to create your dream pin, what would it be?

Pizza Pins

More often than not, the breadth of pin designs and variations created around a particular subject or theme is a great indicator of our level of obsession with the topic, and there are few things human beings are more passionate about than their food—especially their pizza.

The pin game's devotion to the almighty cheese slice is second to none. Do you prefer a pizza slice or a whole pie? How about a vegan pizza? A space-themed pizza? A zombie-themed pizza? Your favorite animal eating a pizza? Yup, there's a pin for all that and much more!

THIS PAGE: Friends Por Vida by Summer Por Vida; Pizza Donut from the Simpsons Man. **OPPOSITE:** Pizza from Wild Tiger Pins; Pizza Boxes and Pizza Cone from All Day I Dream About Pizza (ADIDAP).

Animal Pizza Pins

Why have only one of your favorite things when you can have two? Design mash-ups between multiple favorite topics are a common practice for creators in the pin game, and pizza pins are no different. Possibly one of the most popular design topics besides pizza involves internet-favorite cats, so pizza-cat mash-up pins are inevitable.

Erik Patton from All Day I Dream About Pizza: "All Day I Dream About Pizza (ADIDAP) specializes in everything pizza with a side of skateboarding and cats. A few years ago, not too many people were making pizza-related pins, so we thought it would be funny and fun to make them, and now we've sold hundreds of them. We definitely owe a lot to the pin game because we wouldn't be where we are today without the people who support it."

THESE PAGES: Black Pizza Cat from Oh Plesiosaur; others from ADIDAP. PAGES 32-33: 1 Million Spacebucks from ADIDAP and Hoofarded; Pizza Wave and Pizza Skater from ADIDAP; Grab-A-Slice Zombie Pizza Hand, Crimson Crust Pizza Ghost Punk, and Pizza's Not Dead Punk Rocker from Worm Carnevale; Through Thick & Thin from wwwhiteyyy; Pizza Friend from Killer Acid; Rad Pizza from Jad Dovey; Galaxy Pizza from EmeraldSora; Jesus Pizza from Pizzaboyzzz and Buchovision; Pizza Shark and Pizzalangelo from Anthony Petrie Print + Product Design; Skate Slice Pin from Screamer's Pizzeria & Pinlord.

CATS AREN'T THE ONLY PIZZA PIN
MASH-UP OUT THERE. HAVE YOU
EVER WONDERED WHAT A SPACE
PIZZA WOULD LOOK LIKE? HOW
ABOUT JESUS IN PIZZA FORM?
LUCKILY FOR US, PIN MAKERS ARE
CREATING SOME OF THE MOST
BIZARRE AND OUTLANDISH PIZZA
MASH-UPS OUT THERE.

Worm Carnevale from Scumbags & Superstars: "I knew I wanted to create a pizza friendship set, but I didn't want to just simply put some pizza slices together. I thought it would be fun if each friend was portrayed by an undying zombie hand holding their slice. . . . As for the packaging, I jetted over to a restaurant-supply store in NYC and slapped a custom sticker I made on a mini pizza box."

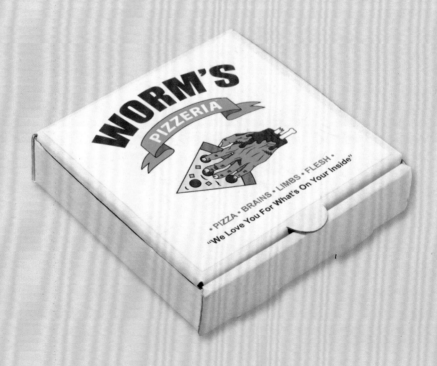

Other Food Pins

From our go-to guilty pleasures like pizza and donuts to the most esoteric interpretations of how food can be depicted visually, there's a food pin for everyone.

Anthony Petrie Print + Product Design: "The idea for our food pins came from something as simple as just wanting to combine two of my favorite things, dinosaurs and food."

THIS PAGE: Nachosaurus from Anthony Petrie Print & Product Design; Skate Dog from Eric F. Dot & Pinlord.
OPPOSITE: Moon Food and Team Alfredo from Dorrarium; Spam Musubi and Kebab Stick from Rolling Death Maui; Guacamole Chaser from NerdPins; Nachos Rule from Jad Dovey & Alex Strangler; French Bread from Lizzie Darden; Poor Little Ramen from Robot Dance Battle.

Brittany Ketterman from Pretty Candy Pin Company: "My first pin design was my aquafaba pin. It was such a risk, I felt, doing something so incredibly niche, but I loved my illustration and I felt really good about it. A good tip for anyone starting in the pin game is to believe in their work, because it makes it so much easier to market when you yourself are excited about and in love with your art. But that risk I took ended up paying off wonderfully, as the vegan community has been absolutely the most supportive of my work, and has definitely helped steer me in the direction I'd like the shop to go. Deciding to listen to my gut and go risky from the start was the best decision I could have made."

OPPOSITE: All pins from Pretty Candy Pin Company. PAGES 40—41: Hot Coffee from Inner Decay; Diner Coffee from Champs Diner & Pinlord; Iced Coffee from Pinlord; Champs Shake from Champs Diner; Tiki Drink from NerdPins; Mickey Mouse Pancake from High Five Pins; Cherry on Top from Dorrarium; Peach from Robin Eisenberg; Vegan Donut Warrior from NerdPins; Brrr from Jad Dovey.

DON'T FORGET, THERE'S NOTHING BETTER THAN WASHING DOWN A GOOD MEAL WITH YOUR FAVORITE BEVERAGE.

Pop-Culture Pins

The pin movement was largely fueled by fans' unfulfilled desire to get their hands on something physical to honor the pop-culture moments they feel nostalgic about—so it makes sense that movie, TV, music, and video game references are some of the most popular pins out there. What's that all-time favorite hit TV show or movie you've been obsessed with for years? What if you could create your own take on that obscure quote, scene, or favorite character you and your equally obsessed friends always refer to? Well, you can in pin form!

Ryan De La Hoz from PSA Press: "We try to instill a deeper meaning to a lot of the pins we produce, even if on the surface it's a simple pop-culture reference. An example would be using our *Apocalypse Now* wall pins to address the state of the nation. We cull inspiration from the past and present it with a wink and a nod to the present day."

Book Pins

OR IF ANALOG MEDIA IS MORE YOUR THING, THERE ARE BOOK PINS OUT THERE FOR YOU TOO.

THESE PAGES: All pins from Ideal Book Shelf.

LD WAS HERE

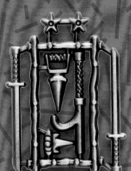

SAN JUNIPERO

COME AND STAY!

I'M NOT FAT. I'M CULTIVATING MASS

Television Pins

Few things are as dear to our hearts as the TV shows we grew up watching. We've all experienced that hole that's left when they go off the air. To remember and honor what these shows meant to us, many pin makers create designs that revere and parody the most iconic TV moments, as well as the obscure ones that only true fans would recognize.

OPPOSITE: I'm Not Fat from Pinch Company; Dharma Initiative from Adam Vass; TMNT Weapon Rack from PSA Press; That Was a Hoot from JUNK-O; San Junipero from Pinlord; LD Was Here from ADIDAP. **THIS PAGE:** Frank Warthog from Pinch Company.

Movie Pins

What was the first movie you remember making an impression on you as a kid? We all have that one line, character, or scene that's etched in our consciousness forever, and there's nothing like meeting someone else who is as obsessed as you are. Making pins that pay homage to those films that have shaped our lives is like lighting a beacon and shining it out to the world in hopes of finding someone who was shaped by it too.

Jensen Karp & Melissa Stetten from Patti Lapel explain: "We try to make pins based on obscure things that happened in some of our favorite movies. We could easily make a Cher from *Clueless* pin saying 'as if,' *but* remember the even more awesome moment when Brittany Murphy said 'rollin with the homies?' We try to invoke those memories in our pins. Not obvious, but weirdly memorable moments. It still amazes us when a pin of Ace Ventura bursting out of a rhino's ass sells out in a week."

OPPOSITE: When Nature Calls, Gloria, Apollo Sweater, and Penny Break from Patti Lapel; Raptor Claw and Apocalypse Now from PSA Press; Zoltar from NerdPins; Creep from Suspect Ltd.

Nostalgia Pins

Life can be scary and unpredictable. Is that the driving force behind our sentimental longing for all of the people, places, and things that remind us of a seemingly simpler, more pleasant past? Whatever the meaning is, our love for all things nostalgic has never been stronger, and through the creative empowerment that enamel pin making has enabled, we now have an unprecedented glimpse into what memories people hold dear enough to make into collectible art.

Marisa Ravel from Laser Kitten: "I wanted to merge my love of fashion with everything I loved growing up in the '80s and '90s. I like to say if Lisa Frank and Courtney Love had a baby, it would be Laser Kitten."

OPPOSITE: Dreamy Controller and Floppy Disk from Free Radicals; Fruit Punch and 90's Computer from Laser Kitten. **THIS PAGE:** All pins from Laser Kitten.

Horror Pins

Horror pins, like horror films, are created to do one thing: scare the living crap out of you, but in a good way. There's nothing like a little jolt of dread to make you feel alive, and horror fanatics have taken to pins to bring their favorite obscure films of the '60s, '70s, '80s, and '90s back from the dead.

Kellie Taylor from Creepy Co.: "Back in March of 2015, I was working a job I hated, and I really just needed something to do after hours that would take my attention away from having to go back in the next day. The first pin I made sold out in a few days, so I moved on to the next design, which is now our company logo: the plastic vampire fangs "Chompers." That pin sold out equally fast. After the first two pins were made, I started to think about my personal interests and what images were very underrepresented in this new hobby or category of collectorship. It didn't take long before I landed on horror as our focus. That's what Creepy Co. grew out of: filling a void for horror/creepy/weird enamel pins!"

THIS PAGE: All pins from Creepy Co. **OPPOSITE:** Young Bobby Myers from Jad Dovey; all others from Creepy Co.

Music Pins

Die-hard music enthusiasts from all over the globe use pins as the medium to pay homage to those artists, songs, albums, and instruments that have made an impact in their lives. Whether it's your favorite '80s New Wave band or that one synthesizer you've always loved, music is alive and well in the pin game.

Benjie Escobar from Louder than Bombs: "Music has always played a huge role in my life. I grew up listening to certain artists/groups and slowly began making merchandise for friends' bands. I've always wanted to do 'my version' of products that existed back then, so if anything it's just me doing something nice for my child self."

THIS PAGE: Karma Police from PSA Press. OPPOSITE: MP3, Dead, and No from Suspect Ltd.; Ian Curtis Headstone from PSA Press; Soul Slam SF XII from Peabe; Makaveli from Good Dope Supply Co.; Bohemian Catsody from Katie Abey Design; Synth Keyboard from Charming Afternoon; Burn Down the Disco from Louder than Bombs; Figure 8 from Battle Born Pins.

Political Pins

The pin game isn't all about pizza and cats. The creation and dissemination of enamel pins as political propaganda has been a part of the industry since its early days. But now, with the democratization of access to production and distribution, private citizens use enamel pins as a tool to express their dissatisfaction with the political establishment and the status quo—with a bit of tongue-in-cheek fun, of course.

Activist pin makers have raised thousands of dollars for their favorite causes by selling pins, channeling the pin movement's power toward what they'd like to change in the world. What cause would you make pins for?

Laura Guardalabene and Nicholas Peters from JUNK-O: "There's just too much going on today to *not* make pins that can help raise a little awareness. It's provided an opportunity to speak our minds, champion our beliefs, and raise money for nonprofit organizations that are doing great work."

THIS PAGE: No Problem from Suspect Ltd.; Nagasaki from wwwhiteyyy. OPPOSITE: Fake News and Net Neutrality from JUNK-O; Stay Woke and Putin Clown from Pinlord; Stop Killing Animals from NerdPins; Hulking Debt from PSA Press.

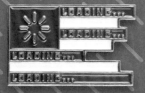

stay woke.

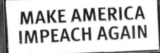

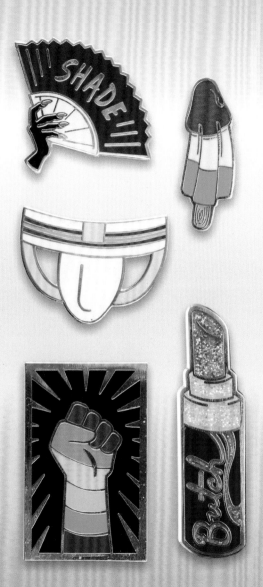

Stevie Hannigan from GAYPIN': "When lapel pins started making their comeback, we loved using them to show a more personal side of who we were, but there weren't enough gay pins on the market to satisfy our cravings. With the current social climate in the world, I think people feel an added urgency to be outwardly visible as LGBTQ+ or an ally to our community. Gay men are still being put in concentration camps. More than twenty-five trans people were killed in the United States in 2017. The suicide rate for LGBTQ+ is more than three times the average of that of their straight peers. Forty percent of homeless youth identify as LGBTQ+ because they are often kicked out of their homes when they come out. We want folks wearing our pins to look down at their lapel and feel their community there with them at any time of feeling alone or uncomfortable. And on top of all of this, they're just really fucking cute and fun to wear."

THIS PAGE: All pins from GAYPIN'. OPPOSITE: Impeach Trump Pop Art Lips from Hello Sailor Tees; Dump Trump Now and Not My President from Pin Bitch; Rainbow T. Rex from Oh Plesiosaur; Golf Much from Sullivan Pin Shop; Trumpig from Dysalexic's Secret Stash; Trump Lives from Creepy Co.; Make America Impeach Again from Little Star Things; Impeach Trump from Pinlord.

Female-Empowerment Pins

Solidarity, protest, and empowerment among female pin makers and their allies have given rise to one of the most inspiring and positive movements within the community. Pin maker Jacie Anderson-Coovert from @bandofweirdos puts it best when talking about why she makes pins that address female empowerment:

"Wearing pins that are centered around female empowerment builds a sense of camaraderie and strength. You can walk by a complete stranger on the street and feel connected without saying a word. This sense of sisterhood is so important in helping us build confidence individually and as a gender.

"We've been made to feel weak and small, but the more we speak up for women's rights, the more change will happen. Pins are a wonderfully accessible way into sharing what you believe."

WEARING WHATEVER THE HELL I WANT

MY BODY MY BIDNISS

MY BODY CHOICE

Nevertheless, She Persisted

BEHOLD MY FEMINIST AGENDA

I'M NOT SORRY ABOUT YOUR FRAGILE MASCULINITY

ya who cares

DELICATE AND STRONG

BOSS BABES UNITE

Too Pretty For This Shit

Cultural Pins

There are some references no one except the people who grew up in the same small town, city, or country can understand. Creatives from all backgrounds have joined the pin world to showcase the culture they come from and honor their personal backgrounds.

David Aguirre from PINetration: "I played in a band for many years. I've always been into buttons and pins. In the punk rock scene, there was never anything that catered to Latinos. One day I started looking for a Cantinflas pin to put on my jacket and realized it didn't exist. It occurred to me that this would be a good way to share things about the Latino culture: by making pins with Latino concepts. Now, whether you want a Buki pin, a Huarache pin, or a pin of an ice cream cart, I feel responsible for making sure you have access to that."

THIS PAGE: Cries in Spanish from Cristo Saez; all others from PINetration.

Clifford Graham from Rolling Death Maui: "I was born and raised on Maui. Lots of the Rolling Death Maui team was too. Most of the pins I make are Hawaii-inspired in one way or another. Some obvious, like the Titty-Shaka or Poke pin, but other ones like characters from classic surf movies (*North Shore*) might not make sense to people outside of Hawaii but are very much what we're all about."

THIS PAGE: All from Rolling Death Maui.

Feelings Pins

Why wear your thoughts on your sleeve when you can wear them on your lapel? Wearing that one pin that exactly expresses how you woke up feeling this morning will likely say more to the world than words ever could.

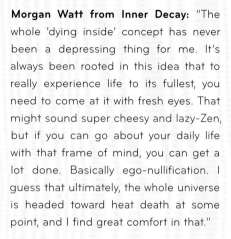

Morgan Watt from Inner Decay: "The whole 'dying inside' concept has never been a depressing thing for me. It's always been rooted in this idea that to really experience life to its fullest, you need to come at it with fresh eyes. That might sound super cheesy and lazy-Zen, but if you can go about your daily life with that frame of mind, you can get a lot done. Basically ego-nullification. I guess that ultimately, the whole universe is headed toward heat death at some point, and I find great comfort in that."

Ultimately, we share our feelings in the hope that it might help us be just a little bit happier . . .

THIS PAGE: No Exit from Suspect Ltd; Jar of Fucks from Katie Abey Design; No Thanks from Cousins Collective; A Happy Ending from ADAMJK; Dying Inside, Nihilism, and Destroy Me from Inner Decay. OPPOSITE: Lowered Expectations from NerdPins; Van Goth from the DNA Life; Keep Out and R.I.P. Feelings from Inner Decay; Welp from Pretty Candy Pin Company; Anxiety Is My Co-Pilot from Tough Times Press; My God You Suck from Paige Vickers & Pinlord; the Human Experience from Plaaastic & Pinlord.

Vices Pins

Our vices are often illegal, but making pins about them isn't! People are very passionate about their drugs and other vices, even if sometimes they can't communicate it openly.

Max McKenna from Roll the Vice: "I make vice-related pins because, as my tagline says, 'Everybody has one.' Whether it be drugs, sex, TV, or a whole other menagerie of things, we all have that one escape. The idea behind Roll the Vice was to create an exclusivity not found with other pins, incorporating realistically detailed elements that would only be understood by people in the know. The glitter caught in the upper corners of the seal on the Baggie pins, the different types of knots seen in the Corner Sack and the 40 Sack pins, and the seemingly innocent, light-orange-colored chunks in an ovular shape seen in the Molly Capsule pin are some of the intricate details that make the pins unique. Roll the Vice is not here to condone, encourage, or criticize drug use; Roll the Vice is here to represent the inebriated, medicated, empowered, and even-keeled."

THIS PAGE: Baggie and Molly Capsule pins from Roll the Vice; Just Lit It from Tough Times Press; Lean from Good Dope Supply Co. OPPOSITE: Nature Makes Me Happy from BaeBeeCoo & Pinlord; High Flyer from Catsneeze; You Light Up My Life from Pinch Co.; Xany Bar from Lil Bullies Club; Ride the Lightning from Jonny Pin Co. & Pinlord; Happy Bong from Killer Acid; Sweet Dreams and Acid from King Drippa.

happy nature makes me happy

HIGH FLYER

YOU LIGHT UP MY LIFE

XANAX

MDMA

Sweet Dreams

DONT EVER TRY Acid

Skull Pins

Skulls have a universal appeal that never goes out of style, and the pin game has created its own unique spin on the art form. For symbolism, for social commentary, or simply because they look badass, makers have embraced the skull as a versatile, cool symbol.

Garth Warner from ColdToes: "Artists have been using skulls for forever to represent mortality, and I think a lot of people are in touch with that. The fear of death and doing everything you want to do before you die is a pretty universal notion; that explains why the symbolism of a skull is so common with a lot of artists. I never intended to release so many pins and patches with skulls; it just sort of happened because that's what I've always been into."

OPPOSITE: Death Rainbow from Jad Dovey; Jackie Skeleton from tinycup needleworkds & Lost Lust Supply Skull Brick from PSA Press; Love You to Death from Lost Lust Supply; Deepest Sleep from ColdToes & Catsneeze; all other pins from ColdToes.

Plant Pins

Plants are a great way to spruce up your home, your office, or your lapel. These faithful companions not only provide us with the oxygen we need to live, but also serve as a great source of inspiration, frustration, friendship, and joy in our everyday lives. Some of us choose to honor them by immortalizing them in pin form, like **Annie Narrigan and Vicky Florio from Life Wife Press:** "Neither of us have much of a green thumb, but we love to look at plants, so it made sense to create a plant someone could have with them at all times that they didn't need to water."

THIS PAGE: Terrazzo Planter from Life Wife Press.
OPPOSITE: Sweaty Palm from Tula Plants & Design; Terrazzo, Noodle, and Squiggle planters from Life Wife Press; You Had Me at Aloe from Pinlord; Peekaboo Baby Sloth and Prickly Pear Cactus from Dorrarium.

YOU HAD ME AT

ALOE

Outdoors Pins

Albert Einstein once said, "Look deep into nature, and then you will understand everything better." The same applies to pins.

Charlie Wagers from Lost Lust Supply: "The nature theme that is consistent through many of our pins simply comes from our love for the outdoors. We're making items that we'd wear ourselves, which hopefully resonate with our friends and also our customers."

THESE PAGES: All pins from Lost Lust Supply.

Animal Pins

Like the animal kingdom itself, each animal-inspired pin, with its own unique set of characteristics, quirks, and flair, is an example of the beauty that beings on this planet are capable of creating.

Natelle Quek from Natelle Draws Stuff: "I wrote to Sir David Attenborough and Stephen Fry in mid-2017, and with the letters, I enclosed one of my Bird-of-Paradise pins for David Attenborough, and for Stephen Fry, a Kakapo pin (in reference to their presentation of BBC's *Planet Earth* and *Last Chance to See*, respectively). A few months after posting, I received a handwritten thank you letter from both of them! And you know I totally laminated those letters too because they needed to be immortalized, and because I'm very good at getting coffee and tea stains on important things."

THIS PAGE: Peony Manatee and Kakapo from Natelle Draws Stuff. OPPOSITE: Ollie from In Front of Apple & Pinlord; Whale-derness, Octopus, and Vampire Squid from Oh Plesiosaur; Shark from Strike Gently Co.; MoonMoth from Northern Spells; Danzig Ram from Steve Seeley & PSA Press.

Cat Pins

People love them, the internet loves them, and the pin game loves them, too. Whether it's their inescapable furry cuteness or an admiration for how little they care about our presence, there's no denying that we feel very passionate about cats.

Katie Cullen from Katie Abey Design explains the appeal: "I like the idea of cat pins, as they show other cat people that you are a cat person too. It's like a secret club. If someone likes cats then I know that I am 99 percent likely to get on well with that person."

THIS PAGE: Taco Cat from Katie Abey Design; Pizza Cat from Natelle Draws Stuff. OPPOSITE: Fat Cat Appreciation Club from Studiocult.co; Napping Cat from Northern Spells; Purrmaid from Oh Plesiosaur; Cats Hate You from Pinlord; all others from Natelle Draws Stuff.

Alien Pins

Part of being a human on this Earth is looking up at the sky and asking ourselves whether we're alone in this universe. The pin game seems to think we're not.

Laura Guardalabene and Nicholas Peters from JUNK-O: "We binge on sci-fi, *The X-Files*, and crazy UFO documentaries in shameful amounts. It's borderline embarrassing. Making these pins helps us connect with people that are just as weird as we are. Honestly, it's probably our only way of finding friends."

THIS PAGE: The Truth is Out There and Teensy Alien Head from JUNK-O; Masters of Disguise from High Five Pins; Reptilian from Killer Acid; Looking for Love from Tough Times Press; Alien Beer Abduction from Laura Palmer's Dead & Pinlord; Ancient Alien from Suspect Ltd.; Crop Circles from NerdPins; I Still Believe from Band of Weirdos.

Internet Pins

Frank Hughes from High Five Pins: "The best memes have a universal appeal; they allow people to express a myriad of expressions that are instantly relatable. For the most part, they solely exist in a digital space. To be able to physically manifest them into a wearable statement like pins, to us, is one of the ultimate means of expression."

THIS PAGE: Memes and .gif Master from Pinlord; 10/10 Would Not Recommend from Plaaastic & Pinlord; Heart Emoji from Hailee Lautenbach & Pinlord; David from High Five Pins; Help Me I Am in Hell from Tough Times Press.

Art Pins

The pin game wouldn't exist without the independent artists who saw enamel pins as a new medium through which they could share their art with the world. They are that perfect memento that is not only cost efficient and straightforward to produce, but also easy to store, and more importantly, an effective way for art aficionados to support the artists they love and not break the bank. It's been a reliable source of income for many artists, and at times, a great first product that has enabled talented creatives to start earning an income and do more of what they are passionate about.

OPPOSITE: 2 Cute 2 Care and Born to Lose from Gory Bastard & Pinlord; Put On a Happy Face and Teenage Lobotomy from Killer Acid; Then and Now from ADAM JK; Dragon from Robin Eisenberg; Third Eye Cat from Shane Bugbee; Tragicomedy from Ava Samii & Tough Times Press; Mr. Universe from Toma Pegaz & Pinlord.

Adam J. Kurtz from ADAMJK: "I try to think of what I make as tools for people to communicate what is often hard to say, whether it's an apology, a pep talk, or a confession. If my pins can provide a little extra encouragement or support, then I've made something to be proud of."

Robin Eisenberg: "Pin making changed my art career in a huge way! Lots of companies who've gotten in touch with me have found me via my pins or even by seeing someone wearing a pin at their office. It's sort of like having business cards all over the world. Yay for enamel pins!"

Rob Corradetti from Killer Acid: "I challenge people to make their own original intellectual thoughts, even if riffing off pop culture is your jam. There is a way to do it that honors the original source material but also creates a fun new thing. Aim high!"

Sierra Siemer: "My roots are in the digital world, experimenting with glitch art and animations. A print is a big purchase, but a pin is like a gateway drug into art. It's easy to connect with people in this way, and then hopefully they'll like the other things you make as well."

Louie Symons from Gory Bastard: "My art's main purpose has always been on some level to make people laugh. Pins are a perfect platform for me because people can now wear my art for others to interact with outside of the confines of social media."

Shane Bugbee: "Most of my pins are a projection of my political self. My politics are of the free-thought movement, the freedom to think and be and express who and what you are from moment to moment. I like to push forward the idea that humans live an individual, nuanced, and circumstantial existence; we don't think alike, nor do we all process information the same."

Garry and Arlene Booth from Pin Museum: "Pins naturally appeal to artsy folks, as well as avid collectors. With an art-school and gallery background, it seemed like a natural evolution of the things we are interested in. Pins seemed to us the perfect medium to express a unique class of interests, as well as support something we all love."

THIS PAGE: 2 Cute 2 Care from Gory Bastard & Pinlord; Kyle Platts from Kyle Platts & PSA Press; Cheat You Fair from Shane Bugbee. OPPOSITE: All from Pin Museum.

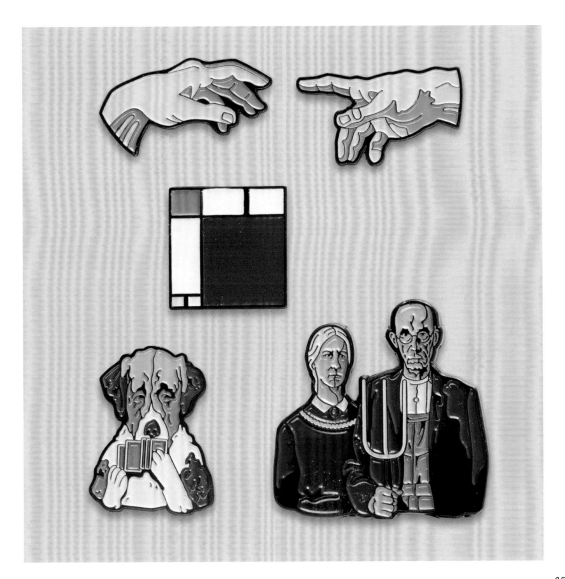

Innovative Pins

Some creative pin artists look to experiment with the boundaries that the pin medium itself has to offer.

Victoria and Sarah from Plain Pins: "Creating a language in color is central to Plain Pins. The simplicity of the pins means they can be worn by many, irrespective of style or taste."

THIS PAGE: All from Plain Pins. **OPPOSITE:** Breakdancer from Good Dope Supply Co.

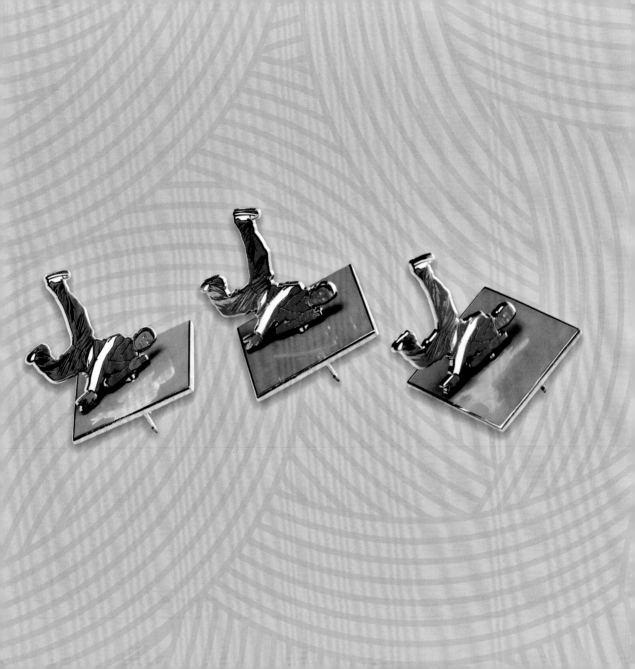

Jimmy McMillan of Suspect Ltd.: "For me, the process of creating an interactive pin is completely context-specific—whether a design incorporates spinning or spring-mounted elements, chains or glow-in-the-dark enamel, it's employed because it's essential to a design, rather than used arbitrarily.

"The hypnotist's pocket watch in my Hypnotic Terror pin set involves a chain on which the watch fob hangs, in order to produce the same pendulum-like effect as its full-sized counterpart. The spinning functionality of the Steal Your Illusion pin is employed specifically for the moiré effect that it generates against its contrasting base. The Mood pin appropriated a reshuffled version of the logo for the PC game *Doom* and employed thermochromic paint to render it a color-changing 'mood ring' pin. I've found interactive elements to be most effective when their inclusion is integral to the concept or mechanics of the piece it references."

THIS PAGE: Cryo-Can by Patti Lapel; others by Suspect Ltd. **OPPOSITE:** Indecisive Spinner from ADAMJK; Woodchipper from Creepy Co.; Nunchuck and Crushed from Suspect Ltd.; Fidget Spinner from High Five Pins; Butterfly Knife from Peabe & Reppin Pins; Stripper from Good Dope Supply Co.; Eye Rolls for Gender Roles from Band of Weirdos; Old Web Ass from Killer Acid.

Collaboration Pins

Collaborations between pin artists and larger brands have resulted in fruitful partnerships that have spurred creative designs and offered more opportunities to budding artists.

Pintrill, an enamel-pin-focused lifestyle brand founded by Jordan Roschwalb in spring 2014, has collaborated with major brands like Adidas, Levi's, Champion, and many others as well as had their designs stocked in more than one thousand stores including Colette, Opening Ceremony, the Museum of Modern Art, and many others. In 2016, they also opened a flagship store in Brooklyn, NY, dedicated exclusively to enamel pins, a first in the pin game.

"I started Pintrill in April of 2014. I wanted to create a one-size-fits-all item that could showcase individuality and appeal to everyone. I always collected pins as a child, so I decided that pins was a great choice—unisex and accessible, one size fits all. Initially, I just wanted to pay my rent. At some point it became so much more than that—I wanted to create a global pin brand. I wanted to be the Nike of pins," says Roschwalb.

Another pin-focused company is **Strike Gently Co.**, founded by Charlie Ambler in October 2015, which has since released over two hundred enamel pin collaborations with up-and-coming illustrators and artists. This collaborative ethos has established a platform for artists to discover new audiences and preexisting fans to purchase products made by their favorite artists.

"I do artist collaborations because without them I wouldn't want to do this job. I don't have much artistic talent myself, but I love art history and the evolution of imagery, so seeing young artists doing incredibly original work inspires me. Being the intermediary between artists and customers who may otherwise never encounter their work is fun too. Everyone benefits. If you don't have that mutually beneficial atmosphere in business, it's no fun," Ambler explains.

THIS PAGE: Eyes from Nemanja Bogdanov & Strike Gently Co. OPPOSITE: Himighi from Kim Mikhi & Strike Gently Co., Switchblade and Shark from Nemanja Bogdanov & Strike Gently Co., Tiger from Pitta Kim & Strike Gently Co., Coffin and Cat from Hwang Boi 1991 & Strike Gently Co.

Join the Pin Game

MAKE YOUR OWN PINS!

Now that you've seen the some of the best and most inspiring pins from around the world, how about making your own? With pins, no longer do you have to accept what big brands and retailers want to sell to you. No longer do you need anyone's permission to start your own creative business. No longer does the likelihood of your success depend on how much money you have or whom you know. Through enamel pins, you can create the art and accessories *you* want to own. Your level of success depends on how skilled you are at creating products people love and your commitment to getting them out into the world. All you need to get started is the internet, a smartphone, and less than a couple hundred bucks.

If you notice even the slightest bit of excitement within yourself when you think about the possibility, I encourage you take the leap and try it out. Make your own pin! Empower the creative voice inside of you and start earning an income, or just make an awesome gift, by producing a long-lasting treasure you and others will love.

The process of getting a pin idea produced may seem daunting at first, but believe me, it's not. Anyone can do it, and it's a lot easier than you think.

Pin Design

The first and, in my opinion, most fun step in the pin production process is deciding what you're going to make. Have you ever dreamed of having a pin of your face on a unicorn's body? Maybe a pin of that one piece of art you've made that you haven't shared with the world? How about a pin of your favorite home-cooked meal your mom used to make for you? The possibilities are endless! If you can design it, it can be made into a pin.

So, how do you choose what to make? There is no step-by-step tutorial for this part of the process, but there is one essential principle that might help you come up with ideas: Design something that you are passionate about. There are hundreds of pins out there about emojis or cats or pop-culture references. Avoid creating a design of something popular just because you think people would like to buy it. More likely than not, it won't sell well because you'll be competing with the hundreds, if not thousands, of other similar pins.

Instead, focus on inventing a design that *you* will adore. The more personal and specific, the better. There are millions of people interested in pins, and you'll always find someone who shares the same passion for some obscure topic that you love too. Create the pin for that person—and for yourself.

Expert Advice

Bryan "Peabe" Odiamar from Peabe: "Do pins you want for yourself. Otherwise you might get stuck with pins you hate and have to stare at daily until they're gone. Go out and create!"

Ryan De La Hoz from PSA Press: "We believe that the smaller you can make a pin while still being readable and recognizable, the better it is. It is quite easy to have incredible detail in a massive three-inch pin, which, at that size, is entering brooch territory. It is more difficult and rewarding for us to design our pins with as much detail as we can, as small as we can."

Kammy Nguyen from Free Radicals: "I remember fighting with myself about whether I should design stuff that would appeal to people or make things I truly loved. I think my brand started off as a weird struggle between the two and never established a certain aesthetic until much later. [The pin] 'Pop Your Ego' was me trying to illustrate how much of our own ego can inflate/deflate over time. I felt like me even thinking about overall appeal was all in my ego. I started off not knowing anything at all! This 'work' that I do is a huge learning process, and it's humbling to realize that you're not going to have the same desired result as other cooler and more experienced designers/artists."

IMPORTANT NOTE: Respect other people's intellectual property! Copyright infringement is illegal and you run the risk of legal action from the copyright owner if you steal their work and pass it off as your own. Similarly, if you plan to make and sell a pin based on a pop culture property (movie, show, band, etc.) make sure you're following proper copyright and trademark laws.

Jimmy McMillan of Suspect Ltd.: "At times I have some idea in mind—a deviation of a brand logo or reference image—as a means of subverting its original meaning. Other times, I strive for a translation of a recognizable object—a switchblade knife with a rotating blade, an incense packaged in a heat-sealed, smell-proof bag—into the miniaturized pin format, using interactive qualities of the pin format to legitimize that translation. But the overall intent is to get a double take as a response. Whether it's because of a bastardization of a cultural reference or an interactive miniaturization of a recognizable object, the goal is to produce something uncanny and slightly . . . suspect."

Pin Production

Now that you've come up with a design you're passionate about, it's time to prepare the materials and information needed for it to go into production.

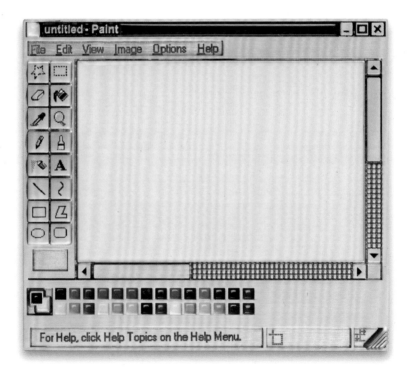

TO PRODUCE A PIN, A FACTORY WILL REQUIRE THE FOLLOWING INFORMATION FROM YOU:

1. A PDF file of the artwork you want to produce.

2. The material you want your pin to be.

3. The size of the pin you want to produce.

4. The quantity of units you want to produce.

5. The number of pin-backs you want your pin to have.

Let's go through what each of these requirements means:

YOUR ARTWORK:

A factory's minimum requirement will be a PDF file of the design you'd like to produce. There are two main ways to prepare your PDF file:

A. CREATE A DIGITAL FILE

If you know your way around one of the many graphic-design software options out there, this one will be a breeze for you. All you'll need to do is draw the outline of the design and specify the colors you'll be using in CMK, RGB, or PMS.

Soft Enamel
- PMS 721
- PMS 464
- PMS 361
- PMS 185
- PMS 291
- White
- Black Dyed
- Die Cut

1.5"

B. SKETCH IT ON PAPER

If you're not savvy with graphic design, you can draw and color a sketch of your idea on a white piece of paper and scan it as a PDF file. Although it's not ideal, most factories offer bare-bones design services and will transform your sketch PDF into production-ready artwork. Proceed with caution here—more likely than not, it won't be high-quality artwork, and that may negatively impact the final product.

If this is your first time making a pin, here are a few design-related strategies that will help:

SIMPLIFY:

Clocking in at around one to two inches in size, pins are a small canvas to work on, so the fewer lines and details you can use to convey an image, the more likely it will translate to a clean and clear pin design.

USE BOLD LINES AND STRONG COLORS:

Again, pins are small, so thin lines and muted colors tend not to stand out when looking at a pin from a distance. Use bold lines and strong colors instead.

AVOID SHADING:

The lines exclusively delimit colors within a pin; this means any type of shading within a color is not possible. Save yourself and the factory some time by not including shading in your pin design.

Pin Material

Although pins can be made from a wide variety of materials, most pin makers stick to two traditional formats: hard-enamel and soft-enamel pins. What's the difference?

HARD-ENAMEL PINS:

Their defining characteristics are the thin metal lines separating each color and their smooth, hard-enamel finish. They are made from die-struck iron metal, which is heated to a high temperature and then polished to create a smooth surface, usually giving them a high-quality, durable feel.

Doris Lu from Dorrarium: "I worked at Ralph Lauren for almost five years before I decided to try something new and start my own venture. I always have had a strong passion for drawing and creating art, and when I came across antique military pins and badges, I knew right away that they were the medium. I spent half a year traveling in China, finding the most suitable factory to make the enamel pins that would meet my standard, researching different types of pin making, and learning about the history of vintage pins versus modern-day pins. Hard enamel is the best way to replicate vintage enamel pins. It's complicated to produce—very labor intensive, with a high defective rate—and it requires lots of attention to detail. But it's all worth the trouble when you see the results—durable, polished, and timeless hard-enamel pins."

SOFT-ENAMEL PINS:

The defining characteristics are their textured pin surface that allows for more detail and a slightly lower cost. They are made from die-struck iron metal, electroplated, and (optionally) epoxy-coated, usually giving them a thinner feel in comparison to hard enamel.

They are both well-tested materials, so whichever one you choose can make for a great pin. Go with whatever style can best communicate your design.

Mike Aknin from Good Dope Supply Co.: "Produce the highest quality pin possible, from the design to the metal you use to the thickness of your pin. This doesn't happen overnight, but through trial and error I think I've reached that point where I'm very proud of the product I produce."

Pin Size

Some people love small pins and others prefer large ones. It's totally up to you! Here are the pros and cons to both.

SMALL PINS:

They are usually between .75 and 1.25 inches wide and long. This makes them more portable, easier to fit onto any surface, and usually lower in cost than larger pins because they use less material. The downside to smaller pins is that they don't allow for as much detail in the design.

LARGE PINS:

Anything larger than 1.25 inches wide or long can be considered a large pin. The size allows for much more detailed designs, but it also limits where they can be pinned. You're likely not going to see many people wearing a two-inch pin on a lapel.

HOW DO YOU DECIDE WHAT SIZE TO USE?

There is no exact formula, but overall, if you're working with a limited budget and have a simple design, smaller pins are likely your best bet. If you want to create a very detailed pin and don't mind paying a higher price, then larger pins are the right option for you.

Rob Corradetti from Killer Acid: "Adham Sallam from Viberaider's Vault had seen a print I had made of this design and contacted me about making it into a pin. I usually produce my own pins, so I was kind of skeptical. Also, it would have to be a *big* pin, like 2.5 inches plus. I'm glad I listened to him though because it opened my eyes to the different world of pins, more of a blinged-out, music-festival jewelry vibe. We ended up making four versions: black metal, edition of 125; all black, edition of 10; silver epoxy, edition of 100; and the coveted gold glitter (no epoxy), edition of 25, which someone had reviewed as 'the Rolls-Royce of pins.' That comment made me laugh. Sometimes it's good to try something different, or to listen to a random person from the internet! Last year I had the fortune of meeting [*The Simpsons* creator] Matt Groening at a book fair and he bought a copy of the pin and a few other things from me, which really brought the journey full circle."

THIS PAGE: Head of Bart from Killer Acid & Viberaider's Vault. OPPOSITE: Frame and Raptor Claw from PSA Press; It's Not a Belt, It's a Title Asshole, from Bad News Browns & Peabe; Lunch from Squid Lords.

Pin Quantity

When it comes to the quantity, you need to take two things into account. First, all factories have a minimum order requirement of one hundred pins, so be prepared for that. Second, the more pins you order, the lower your price per pin will be.

For your first pin order, I'd always recommend sticking to the minimum of one hundred pins and then reordering more if it does well. Most of the time, it's very hard to predict how well your pin will be received, and it's always better to play it safe than order large quantities of a pin no one is buying.

PIN-BACKS:

A pin-back is the needle-like mechanism, usually in the rear section of a pin, that is used to temporarily fasten it to a surface. For first-time pin makers, I always recommend putting two pin-backs on all of your pins. Why? Using only one pin-back will allow your pin to jiggle around wherever you place it, and it'll be a lot more likely to fall off and get lost. There's nothing worse than losing a beloved pin because of faulty pin-back planning. Don't make the mistake I and countless other first-time pin makers have made. Always use two pin-backs.

Find a Factory to Produce Your Pins

Now that you have a PDF of your artwork and you know what material, size, unit quantity, and pin-back quantity (always two!) you're using, you are ready to search for the right factory to produce it. A quick online search for "enamel pin factory" will bring up dozens of suitable producers. Decide which to work with based on whoever gives you the best answers to the following questions:

You send them your artwork with all of your requirements for production.

What will it cost to produce one hundred units of this pin?

(Quick tip: In your message to the factory, make sure to include your artwork, quantity, size, material, and number of pin-backs. It's the information the factory will need in order to give you a price.)

What is your turnaround time?

Once the final pin is produced, can you send me a photo for approval before you ship it out?

Do you accept payment for 50 percent upfront and 50 percent once the final version of the pin is approved and shipped?

All reputable factories are comfortable with these terms, so work with the one that gives you the *best* terms in response to these four questions.

IN MOST CASES, THE PRODUCTION AND COMMUNICATION PROCESS WILL GO SOMETHING LIKE THIS:

They give you a cost, a turnaround time estimate, and final production artwork for your approval.

Once you approve artwork and costs, you pay them 50 percent of the total cost to start production.

They produce the pin for you within the agreed-upon turnaround time.

They give you a tracking number for your shipment, and you receive your pins.

If you're happy with the quality of the final product in the photo, you approve it for shipment and pay them the final 50 percent.

Once the pins are produced, they send you a photo of the final product for your approval.

TA-DA! YOU'VE MADE YOUR FIRST PIN.

Share Your Pins

You've done it! You've produced your first batch of enamel pins, and now it's time you share them with the world. Nothing is better than gifting, receiving, and trading pins with your friends, family, and fellow pin enthusiasts, but if your intention is to start earning an income from your creation, there is one thing you need to do: Just get out there and do it!

Don't let the excuse of not finding the "perfect" way to sell your pins hold you back. The most simple and easily accessible first step is to open up a e-commerce website to list your pins for sale and a Instagram account to market them. Once you have that, also list them on Etsy, Amazon, or any other platform that you think is a good fit for you. Know that it will likely take time, sometimes years, for you to earn a decent income from selling pins, but the only way to give yourself the best shot at success is perseverance. Always test new designs, new selling channels, new ways to reach people! Focus on execution and create pin designs that bring joy to you and those around you. If selling something online isn't your thing, sell them directly to your closest friends, at a store, at a flea market, at school, at work, or anywhere else you can meet people and show them your work, it doesn't matter. All that matters is that you get out there and share your work with the world!

Wear your pins everywhere, and share them through any resources you have available—including your new group of fellow makers and collectors.

The pin game was born from an open and sharing community. If you ever run into trouble or come across problems, you can check out many online resources including my site, pinlordshop.com, where I'm always providing free information on how to build your pin business. If you can't find answers online, don't be afraid to reach out directly to other pin makers and ask them for some guidance. If you are respectful and mindful of people's time, most of them will respond and likely help you by sharing their experience. If you do good work, be certain that one day you'll have other first-time pin makers reaching out to you for some guidance, so make sure to remember that we've all been there and give back.

If you're having trouble selling your pins at first, try giving away and trading pins, getting in touch with pin reposters who can show yours to larger audiences, or cross-promoting pins with other small pin makers. This is not a zero-sum game. Help others, and you'll be helping yourself build a community that will support your business. And who knows, you might end up making some lifelong friendships along the way. Most of us do.

Also, like Trine Sejrup from Northern Spells explains, "Know that to succeed you will have to sacrifice your time. When you do that, you will see you are able to make better things, take more interesting pictures, and learn about timings and how they work best for you." Have confidence in what you make, don't compare yourself to others, and have fun while you're at it.

THIS PAGE: Yes Wine from Occasional Grownup.

CONLUSION

Being part of the pin game is about more than buying, selling, collecting, or making pins. It's about expressing yourself. It's about valuing the power of the human creative spirit and connecting with others who value it too.

If you're reading this book, you're already part of the pin game movement, and for that I thank you from the bottom of my heart. It's because of people like you that the pin world exists.

So if you're interested in helping the movement continue to grow, the best thing you can do is get out there and make pins, collect pins, sell pins, and trade pins. Support the artists who make them, and while you're at it, become one yourself. And have fun with it. Like anything else in life, that's the most important part.

Acknowledgments

Special thanks to the love of my life, Romany, for always providing a safe and loving space in which I can follow my heart. To Padraig, for inspiring me to create @pinlord. To Jimmy, for helping me produce my first pin. And to Worm, for encouraging me to build a business early on.

About the Author

Eduardo Morales, also known as @pinlord on instagram, creates content focused on giving people the knowledge and resources to express their creativity and earn an income through making and selling enamel pins. He currently resides in Brooklyn, New York, living a pin-filled life with his awesome wife, Romany Pope.

Pin Creator Credits

Front Cover Pins: Get Lost and Camper Van from Lost Lust Supply; Gold Tiger from Pitta Kim & Strike Gently Co.; Heart Emoji from Pinlord & Hailee Lautenbach; Dragon from Robin Eisenberg; Boss Babes Unite from Band of Weirdos; Glass Half Full from Paige Vickers & Pinlord; Melted Astronaut from Killer Acid; Skate Dog from Eric F. Dot & Pinlord; Twilight Spiral from Sierra Siemer; Terrazzo Planter from Life Wife Press; Triangle Cat from Natelle Draws Stuff.

Back Cover Pins: Feeling Myself from Robin Eisenberg; Mermaid from Oh Plesiosaur; Cat in a Bag from Pinlord & Nothing on Purpose; Air Cuauhtémoc from PINetration; Nunchuck from Suspect Ltd.; No Thanks Bag from Cousins Collective; Cries in Spanish from Cristo Saez; 90's Computer from Laser Kitten; Noodle Planter from Life Wife Press.

Title Page: Help Me I Am in Hell from Tough Times Press; Then and Now from ADAMJK; Pizza Cat from ADIDAP; Heart Emoji from Hailee Lautenbach & Pinlord; Middle Finger from Robin Eisenberg; Teensy Alien Head from JUNK-O; Third Eye Cat from Shane Bugbee; Gold Tiger from Pitta Kim & Strike Gently Co.; Born to Lose from Gory Bastard & Pinlord; Twin Peaks Zig Zag from Sierra Siemer; Get Lost from Lost Lust Supply; Cries in Spanish from Cristo Saez; Terrazzo Planter from Life Wife Press; GhostPotion from Northern Spells; Spam Musubi from Rolling Death Maui; Guacamole Chaser from NerdPins; Sweaty Palm from Tula Plants & Design; Prickly Pear Cactus from Dorrarium; Keep Out from Inner Decay; Bad Feeling from Poni & Pinlord.

Table of Contents: Bottled Feelings from ADAMJK; If You Want My Future from Band of Weirdos; David from High Five Pins; Retrograde Life from Pinlord; Tin Man Head Poppin' from Killer Acid; 1984 from Ideal Book Shelf; In Order to Die from Suspect Ltd.; Peach the Cat from Michel_e_b & Pinlord; Too Pretty from Lady Love Letter; Daft Punk from Pintrill; Damn Good Joe from Pinlord; My God You Suck from Paige Vickers & Pinlord; Macrame All Day from Macrame Makers; Stay Woke from Pinlord; Fake News from JUNK-O; Mudra from Suspect Ltd.

Introduction: Impeach Trump from Pinlord; Skate Dog from Eric F. Dot & Pinlord; Pizza Cat from ADIDAP; The Hitchhiker's Guide to the Galaxy from Ideal Book Shelf; Sad Bong from Killer Acid; French Bread from Lizzie Darden; Atlas Dunked from Suspect Ltd.; Daft Punk from Pintrill; Friends Por Vida from Summer Por Vida.

Page 8: Get Tuff by Grace Wagner & Pinlord; 10/10 Would Not Recommend from Plaaastic & Pinlord; Cat in a Bag from Nothing on Purpose & Pinlord; Happy Accidents from Brianna Harting & Pinlord; Muretz from Muretz & Pinlord; Diner Coffee from Champs Diner & Pinlord; Alien Beer Abduction from Laura Palmer's Dead & Pinlord; Sweet Tadeo from Hello Hellcat & Pinlord; 80s Lipstick from Design Since 86 & Pinlord; the Pin-Up from Mario Maple & Pinlord; all other pins from Pinlord.

Page 12: Too Pretty from Lady Love Letter; Macrame All Day from Macrame Makers; Hellraiser Homemaker, Satan, Jesus, Kind Abortion, Elephant Baphomet and Creative Class from Shane Bugbee; Infinitely Grateful, Globe, Garbage, NC-17, Atlas Dunked, StealYour_End, and Bad Apple pins from Suspect Ltd.;

Dougie Jones, Damn Good Joe, Impeach Trump, Love Channing, Retrograde Life, Stay Woke, We Sushi Bears, and Xtina pins from Pinlord; Fuck It! Just Do It! from Worm Carnevale; Born to be Mild from Jonny Pin Co.; Butts and Party Soft from Super Team Deluxe; Otomo Capsule from Inner Decay; Pop Your Ego Pack from Free Radicals; RTC from Ryan Travis Christian & PSA Press; Kilroy Skate, Boot, the #pingame from PSA Press; Fun Extinguisher and Personal Jesus from Wild Coma; Relax from ADAMJK; Shinzilla and TOS-T Bot from BB-CRE.8; Fat Cat Appreciation from Studiocult.co; David and MS Paint from High Five Pins; Krustywise and Knuckle Sandwich from Jad Dovey; Melted Astronaut and Tin Man Head Poppin' from Killer Acid; Sweater Platypus and Theremin Cat from Natelle Draws Stuff.

Page 14: Cash Is King, Rainbow Swamp Thing, and Butter from Shane Bugbee; Rude from Rude Collective & Pinlord; Floppy Disc from Free Radicals; Baby Bondage from Lady Love Letter; Holga Camera from Lost Lust Supply; 80s Lipstick from Design Since 86 & Pinlord; Super Au Natural from Ashley Daniliuk &

126

Pinlord; Air POTUS by Peabe.

Page 42: Pins not credited elsewhere: Always Extra Pineapple Pizza from Pretty Candy Pin Company.

Pages 60–61: Badass Quiet Girls from Band of Weirdos; Boss Babes Unite from Band of Weirdos; Behold My Feminist Agenda, I'm Not Sorry about Your Fragile Masculinity, Wearing Whatever the Hell I Want from Fairy Cakes; Nevertheless She Persisted from JUNK-O; Who Cares from Life Wife Press; Middle Finger from Robin Eisenberg; My Body My Choice from Pinlord; Pretty Venus and Too Pretty from Lady Love Letter; Gold Mermaid from Oh Plesiosaur; Grumpy Lingerie from Grumpgrlsam; Resting Witch Face from Inner Decay & the Wing; Titties from Shelby Sells & Pinlord; Delicate and Strong from Northern Spells; Feeling Myself from Robin Eisenberg.

Page 98: Pop Your Ego Pack from Free Radicals and Baby Bondage from Lady Love Letter.

Page 99: Dreamy Controller from Free Radicals; Draw Things from Harold Apples & Lost Lust Supply; Sad Bong from Killer Acid; Shocked, Sauvage, Chains,

and Skeleton from Suspect Ltd.; Oskal from ColdToes; Command Z and Dank Memes from Super Team Deluxe; Metal Up Thy Ass from Shane Bugbee; No Mas from Good Dope Supply Co.; Column Die Cast from PSA Press; Cereal Killers from Little Giants, Giant Shorties & Peabe.

Page 100: All pins from Suspect Ltd.

Page 102: MS Paint from Studiocult.co.

Page 103: MS Paint from High Five Pins; the #pingame from PSA Press.

Page 106: Lounging Lady from Life Wife Press; Adults Only from Suspect Ltd.; Moon Food from Dorrarium; Give Up from Super Team Deluxe; Evil Wink from Tough Times Press; GhostPotion from Northern Spells; Skull Baby and Butter from Shane Bugbee.

Page 109: Skull Squeegee from Lost Lust Supply; Sad Elephant from Katie Abey Design; Cat in a Bag from Nothing on Purpose & Pinlord; Two Cool Dogs from Gory Bastard & Pinlord; Marker from Lil' Bullies; Mariachi from NerdPins; Relax from Squid Lords; Evils of the Flesh from ColdToes; Sad Mac from Sierra Siemer.

Page 110: Switchblade from Nemanja Bogdanov & Strike Gently Co.; Globe, Mood Man, Banned in NYC Switchblade from Suspect Ltd.; Fighting Invisible Battles Medal from Fairy Cakes; Teensy Alien Head from JUNK-O; Bad Feeling from Poni & Pinlord; 90's Cell Phone from Laser Kitten; the Pin-Up from Mario Maple & Pinlord; Rude Dude from Blaire Stapp & Pinlord.

Page 117: MS Paint from High Five Pins; Indecisive Spinner from ADAMJK; Fidget Spinner from High Five Pins; Relax from ADAMJK; Holga Camera from Lost Lust Supply; Bad Mother Fucker from ADIDAP; Theremin Cat from Natelle Draws Stuff.

Title Page: Help Me I Am in Hell from Tough Times Press; Then and Now from ADAMJK; Pizza Cat from ADIDAP; Heart Emoji from Hailee Lautenbach & Pinlord; Middle Finger from Robin Eisenberg; Teensy Alien Head from JUNK-O; Third Eye Cat from Shane Bugbee; Gold Tiger from Pitta Kim & Strike Gently Co.; Born to Lose from Gory Bastard & Pinlord; Twin Peaks Zig Zag from Sierra Siemer; Get Lost from Lost Lust Supply; Cries in Spanish from Cristo Saez; Terrazzo

Planter from Life Wife Press; GhostPotion from Northern Spells; Spam Musubi from Rolling Death Maui; Guacamole Chaser from NerdPins; Sweaty Palm from Tula Plants & Design; Prickly Pear Cactus from Dorrarium; Keep Out from Inner Decay; Bad Feeling from Poni & Pinlord.

Copyright Page: Draw Things from Harold Apples & Lost Lust Supply; Column Die Cast from PSA Press; Command Z from Super Team Deluxe; No Mas from Good Dope Supply Co.

· · · · · · · · · · · · · · · · · · · ·

INSIGHT EDITIONS

PO Box 3088
San Rafael, CA 94912
www.insighteditions.com

Publisher: Raoul Goff
Associate Publisher: Vanessa Lopez
Creative Director: Chrissy Kwasnik
Designer: Ashley Quackenbush
Project Editor: Kelly Reed
Associate Managing Editor: Lauren LePera
Senior Production Editor: Rachel Anderson
Production Manager: Greg Steffen

Photography by Spencer Stucky and Eduardo Morales

Library of Congress Cataloging-in-Publication Data available.

ISBN: 978-1-68383-473-1

ROOTS of PEACE   REPLANTED PAPER

Insight Editions, in association with Roots of Peace, will plant two trees for each tree used in the manufacturing of this book. Roots of Peace is an internationally renowned humanitarian organization dedicated to eradicating land mines worldwide and converting war-torn lands into productive farms and wildlife habitats. Roots of Peace will plant two million fruit and nut trees in Afghanistan and provide farmers there with the skills and support necessary for sustainable land use.

Manufactured in China by Insight Editions

10 9 8 7 6 5 4 3 2 1